SUFFOLK

ROBERT MALSTER

SUTTON PUBLISHING LIMITED

Sutton Publishing Limited
Phoenix Mill · Thrupp · Stroud
Gloucestershire · GL5 2BU

First published 1997

Copyright © Robert Malster, 1997

British Library Cataloguing in Publication Data
A catalogue record for this book is available from the
British Library.

ISBN 0-7509-1449-1

Typeset in 10/12 Perpetua.
Typesetting and origination by
Sutton Publishing Limited.
Printed in Great Britain by
Ebenezer Baylis, Worcester.

Title page: A timeless scene: the watersplash at Kersey.

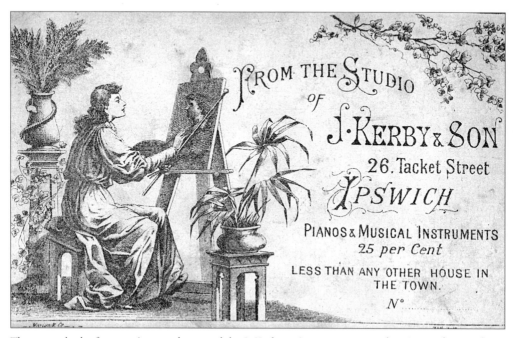

The ornate back of a *carte-de-visite* photograph by J. Kerby & Son, operating in the 1890s. Their studio in Tacket Street was taken over at about the turn of the century by the International Art Company and then by Louis Norman, followed by Leonard Norman.

CONTENTS

'In the Barley-Harvest', one of the Suffolk photographs by Peter Henry Emerson published in his *Pictures of East Anglian Life* in 1888. Emerson, sometimes described as 'the father of naturalistic photography', produced some of the finest Victorian photographs of work on the land.

INTRODUCTION

Until local government was reorganized in 1974 Suffolk had always been a divided county. The separation of west and east went far back into history, to the time when Edward the Confessor gave to Bury St Edmunds Abbey jurisdiction over the eight and a half hundreds known as the Liberty of St Edmund. This was to become West Suffolk. Another abbey, that of Ely, had jurisdiction in five and a half hundreds known as the Liberty of St Etheldreda or the Wicklaw, in the south-east of the county around Woodbridge. In spite of the changes brought about by the dissolution of the monasteries, the Wicklaw continued to be something of a law unto itself until it became part of East Suffolk on the setting up of county councils.

Even after more than twenty years as a unified county, Suffolk still has something of a dual personality; there are still features which enable one to discover the old boundary between east and west. Though Ipswich is now the county town, Bury St Edmunds has administrative offices belonging to the county council and a character that refuses to admit its reduced status.

Although predominantly an agricultural county, Suffolk has throughout its history had its share of industry. In the Middle Ages it was one of the most prosperous areas of the kingdom, for its merchants grew rich on the sale of its woollens, and tourists come today to seek out reminders of the trade that enabled men to seek personal salvation through the building of great churches like those of Long Melford and Lavenham. The weaving trade fell on hard times, but other industries such as malting, engineering and the making of agricultural implements, and the manufacture of clothing have played their part in ensuring that Suffolk has not been solely dependent on farming for employment and wealth.

Suffolk was fortunate in having a surprising number of early photographers, both amateurs and professionals, who delighted in recording the county in which they lived. Their work has left us with a rich heritage of pictures showing much that has disappeared in the past hundred years, and a great deal that has changed.

One of the very earliest amateur photographers to work in the county was Richard Dykes Alexander (1788–1865), a partner in the Ipswich bank of Alexander & Company. A member of a Quaker family, he was related to members of the Dillwyn and Sims families who were involved with the Ransomes in the manufacture of agricultural implements and other things at Ipswich, so it is not surprising that some of his photographs are of steam engines produced by their firm.

To produce a negative he used fine-textured paper which was waxed and then soaked in a solution of potassium iodide. When the paper was to be sensitized it had to be passed through a solution of silver nitrate, washed in distilled water and dried between sheets of blotting paper.

Long exposures were needed with this process, sometimes a quarter of an hour or even more. The disadvantage was that people passing by did not appear on the completed picture, but an advantage was that the photographer could appear in his own photograph by removing the lens cap, walking round and sitting down in the field of view, keeping very still for the length of the exposure and then getting up to replace the lens cap at the end of the time. It is possible that some pictures showing Richard Dykes Alexander himself were taken in this way.

Many photographs taken in the 1850s and 1860s by Alexander surfaced in 1978 when they were sent

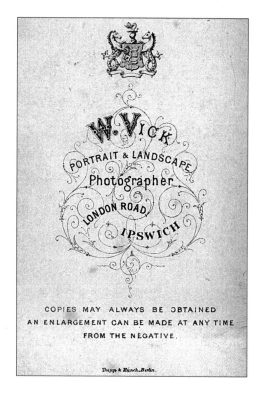

The back of a *carte-de-visite* portrait photograph by William Vick (1833–1911), who took over the Ipswich business of William Cobb *c*. 1870.

to Sotheby's Belgravia for inclusion in a sale of photographic images and related material. Fortunately it was possible for Suffolk Record Office to acquire some of these early pictures, and I have been privileged to include a number of these.

An Ipswich professional artist, Robert Burrows (1810–83), was another who espoused photography in the 1850s, possibly seeing it as an aid to his painting but more likely, on the evidence of what remains, enjoying the new medium for its own sake. An album of small prints made by him is also in the Suffolk Record Office.

Several of the photographs in the early part of this book were taken by an influential amateur, George Christopher Davies (1849–1922), a young Shropshire-born solicitor who was attracted to East Anglia by the lure of the Broads, of which he had read in an article in *The Field*. 'Part of the equipment of a yacht is a photographic camera,' he wrote in 1883, and he and some cruising friends seem to have made good use of theirs while sailing the Broadland waterways. Davies himself published a series of photogravures in the 1880s as well as illustrating his own books.

By 1879 there were no fewer than thirty-one professional photographers, one woman among them, listed in Kelly & Company's *Post Office Directory of Suffolk*, but photography had by then passed its infancy. The home-made paper negative and the daguerreotype had largely given way to the glass plate negative and the bromide printing paper.

Among those professionals was William Vick (1833–1911). He arrived in Ipswich in about 1870 to take over the business of William Cobb, who had described himself in the previous decade as a photographic artist. Vick took many portraits in his studio at Barrack Corner, on the junction of Clarkson Street and London Road, but the photographs for which he is best remembered are his views of Ipswich streets which provide a valuable record of changes to the Victorian town.

Some of his pictures purported to show an even earlier Ipswich, for one of the mounted prints which he sold 'at moderate prices', to quote his advertisement, bore the unlikely caption 'Old Butter Market and Queen Street, 1830'; the earliest-known paper negative dates from 1835. Vick appears to have traded very successfully on a wave of late-Victorian nostalgia, for the most popular of his mounted prints were those that showed buildings already demolished to make way for the Victorian buildings we today are only just beginning to appreciate.

Photographic printing was a somewhat time-consuming process in the third quarter of the nineteenth century, for the sensitized paper had to be placed behind the large glass plate in a wooden frame with a hinged back and exposed to sunlight for some considerable time. When the paper was sufficiently exposed (this could be ascertained by opening a hinged section of the wooden frame, since with printing-out paper the image appeared on the paper in increasing density as the exposure increased) it had to be removed from the frame and fixed in 'hypo' for two minutes. Then it had to be thoroughly washed to remove all traces of the chemical, clipped on to a line to dry, and finally mounted on the card on which it was sold.

Such a process proved unequal to the demand in the case of the more popular pictures, as only a single negative was likely to be available. Vick overcame the bottleneck by making a glass positive from the original negative and then using the positive to produce a number of copy negatives that could be used to produce contact prints for sale. With the most popular pictures of all there might be as many as a dozen copy negatives of the same view in use in his studio, as one can discover from the boxes of glass negatives now in the Suffolk Record Office.

A slightly later Ipswich photographer was Harry Walters, who is said to have made his first camera in the 1870s with the aid of bits and pieces such as a cardboard pillbox which he used as a lens holder. By the

An evocative picture of travelling people with a performing bear. In the last century there were many such itinerant performers, including Italian hurdy-gurdy men and German bands. There is a story of one such traveller who with a dancing bear boarded a Lowestoft tram; their appearance up the rear stairs was the cause of all the upper-deck passengers departing hurriedly down the front stairs. Left alone, the bear became bored, so his master brought out his concertina and the bear began to dance, a performance that caused consternation whenever the tram came to a stop; those waiting to board the tram all decided to wait for the next one. Subsequently the management issued an order that no bears were to be allowed to travel on the town's trams in future. (East Anglian Film Archive)

early years of the twentieth century he was in business at premises in Crown Street, Ipswich, from where he soon moved to a shop next to the Running Buck on St Margaret's Plain, where he remained until his death in 1926.

Harry Walters was an entertainer as well as a photographer, obviously a man with a keen sense of humour. Entertainment and photography became inextricably mixed when he indulged in his favourite trick photography, which included taking multiple pictures of himself. As Harry Wilmott, the negro comedian, he was well known on the local stage; when a plinth was erected in Christchurch Park for a statue of Queen Victoria he took a photograph of himself with his banjo standing on the plinth and entitled it 'Harry Wilmott as he appeared before the Queen' – before, that is, Queen Victoria's statue was installed.

It is impossible, of course, to go through the whole list of the county's early photographers. In Stowmarket there was Arthur Bugg, who operated from a small hut in Finborough Road, in Sudbury there were Miss Susanna Berry and Ambrose Copsey, in Haverhill Charles Mizon, and in Bury St Edmunds William Silas Spanton, John William Clarke and William Aston. Even quite small villages like Brockford and Hoxne had their photographers.

With the growing fashion for picture postcards at the beginning of this century it becomes less easy to assign photographs to particular photographers, though some like Fred Jenkins at Southwold and his brother Harry at Lowestoft took care to stamp their names on the cards they sold to holidaymakers and local people alike.

In an advertisement of 1904 the Southwold Jenkins advised amateur photographers, of whom there were by that time a great many, 'Do not send your PLATES and FILMS to an inexperienced Chemist for Development and Printing'; instead he suggested that they should bring them to one who made a speciality of the work. There is even a suggestion that he had a special darkroom for use by amateur photographers.

Charles Emeny and his son Clement at Felixstowe produced photographs of local scenes and local happenings over a period of some eighty years, for Charles was taking photographs as early as 1867, when he was a youngster of eighteen, and Clement retired only in 1950. When the Royal Naval Air Station was established at Felixstowe in 1913 Charles Emeny became friendly with some of the officers there, with the result that he was one of the earliest to take pictures from the air.

Yet all too many photographs cannot be ascribed to any particular man. Who was the photographer who cycled out to Long Melford in about 1912 to take photographs for reproduction as postcards, and left his cycle leaning against a lamp post as he took the pictures? Could it have been Frank Dicks, of 54 North Street, Sudbury, or Thomas Gates, of 1 Station Road, Sudbury? Or could it have been someone from Emeny & Sons, of 8 Gainsborough Street; and was this family any relation of Charles Emeny at Felixstowe?

When one writes a book one should be answering questions, not asking them, but sometimes one has to admit to not knowing the answer. Dating photographs is by no means easy, and there are many pitfalls. One can spend a considerable time searching with a magnifying glass for clues, and then be misled by a mistake in a directory that includes a particular shop long after it had closed, or fails to record a firm that was indeed trading at the time.

The author has made considerable efforts to date the photographs in this book, but having due regard to the perilous nature of the task apologizes in advance for errors the reader may discover.

For help in the compilation and writing of this book the author has to thank the staff of Suffolk Record Office, David Cleveland, Ivan Codd, the East Anglian Film Archive, Haverhill & District Local History Group, Hugh Moffat, Peter Northeast, John Wilton and others too numerous to mention individually who have been generous with information and with the loan of photographs. Those pictures not otherwise acknowledged are from the author's collection; he is mindful that many of these were given to him in the distant past by friends.

THE WAVENEY VALLEY

The impressive walls and bastions of Burgh Castle (now in Norfolk, but until 1974 a part of Suffolk) remain as one of the most outstanding monuments of Roman occupation. This photograph by George Christopher Davies, an amateur photographer and Broads sailor who did much to put the area on the tourist map, dates from c. 1880. When the fort was built in the second half of the third century it faced out on to a broad estuary with a substantial Roman port on the north side at Caister-by-Yarmouth.

The broads were formed in medieval times as peat pits, from which fuel was obtained both for the local salt industry and for monastic establishments such as the cathedral priory at Norwich. Fritton Lake was one of those formed in side valleys rather than in the marshes alongside the main rivers and was later used as a duck decoy for capturing wild ducks for the table. An average take each season was about a thousand duck. This photograph showing the mouth of the decoy pipe is, like the others on succeeding pages, from a series of sixteen negatives taken by G.C. Davies in 1882. As Davies and his companions approached the decoy on their first visit they were given a piece of smouldering turf to carry, the object being to destroy their own scent which would have alarmed the ducks.

The decoyman and the decoy dog, whose job was to arouse the ducks' curiosity and attract them into the pipe, standing by the purse net at the end of the pipe. When the ducks reached this end of the net they were doomed; their necks would be wrung so silently by the decoyman that their fellows outside the pipe would remain unaware of the danger.

Reed screens at the side of the pipe were so angled that seen from the lake they presented a solid wall. The low walls seen in the lower picture were termed 'dog jumps'; the decoy dog would leap over one and disappear, luring the curious ducks further up the pipe towards the fatal purse net at the end.

A cargo-carrying billy-boy on its way upriver to Beccles passes a group of yachts belonging to members of the Yare Sailing Club near the entrance to Oulton Dyke on 3 August 1881. For many years Beccles was a minor inland port, importing grain and coal and exporting malt and flour; there was a short-lived revival of trade in the 1950s when Thames barges brought wheat to Green's mills in the town.

The same billy-boy lying at Beccles Quay a day or two later, seen in another of G.C. Davies' photographs.
A new bridge was under construction at the time to replace the stone one that had existed since at least
the early seventeenth century, and the building operations can be seen in the background.

Three wherries, one of them either newly built or just refitted, lie above the bridge in this view of Beccles from the river, *c.* 1881. Seagoing vessels could not pass under the bridge, but wherries went on upriver to Bungay through a series of locks.

Boater's Hills, seen in a photograph taken *c.* 1904, were at one time a favourite pleasure resort of the people of Beccles. This pleasant spot on the Norfolk bank of the Waveney a mile or so below the town took its name from a boathouse which stood on the riverside; the word boat'us, as pronounced locally, became corrupted to Boater's.

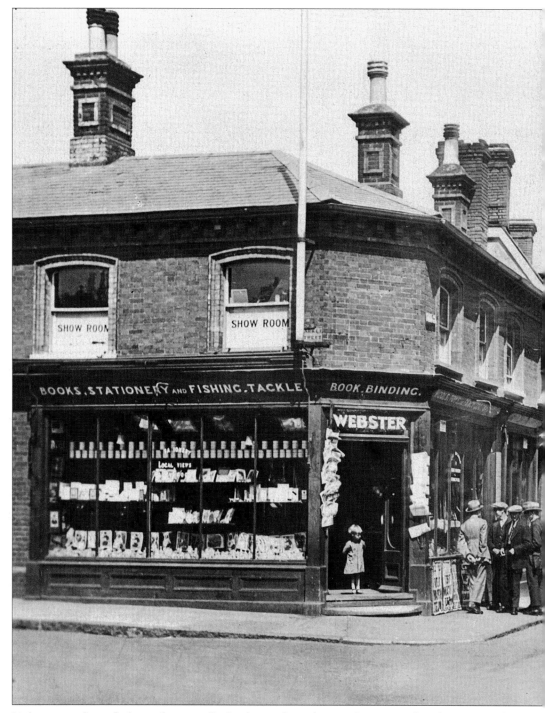

Little groups of men find time for a mardle (local term for a chat) on the corner of Market Street and Smallgate, Beccles, in the early 1920s. Prominent in this view is the stationery shop of Harry Webster, who published a postcard of the scene. Webster had taken over the business carried on for many years by Caleb Chase. On the other side of Smallgate is the White Lion Hotel, which at this time still advertised itself as a posting house; horses could be hired there.

The church of St Michael's at Beccles is unusual in having a detached tower standing near the east end.
When construction of the tower began in the early sixteenth century it was obviously considered unsafe to
build at the west end of the church since so massive a structure might prove unstable at the top of the
steep slope down to Pudding Moor. Impressive as it is, the tower was never completed; there should have
been another stage above what is now the top stage.

Beccles post office in Exchange Square, looking down Smallgate to the stuccoed frontage of the Public Hall at the top of Station Road. Below is a view of Pudding Moor, a street which runs parallel with the River Waveney at the foot of a steep slope down from the town. In this case Moor is equated with marsh rather than heather-clad upland, and Pudding is the local name for a toad.

The Market Place at Bungay, with the tower of St Mary's Church rising above the rooftops. Like its neighbour Beccles, Bungay suffered a severe fire in the seventeenth century and almost all the older buildings were erected following the destruction wrought by the fire. It was at that time that the handsome Butter Cross was erected in the Market Place. On the left of the picture, taken in the 1920s, is the grocer's shop of Brewster & Balls, who as can be seen were also wine and spirit merchants. This picture, taken by a photographer employed by Jarrolds of Norwich, was used to produce a postcard sold by H.W. Short, printer, stationer, bookbinder, bookseller and newsagent at 14 Market Place.

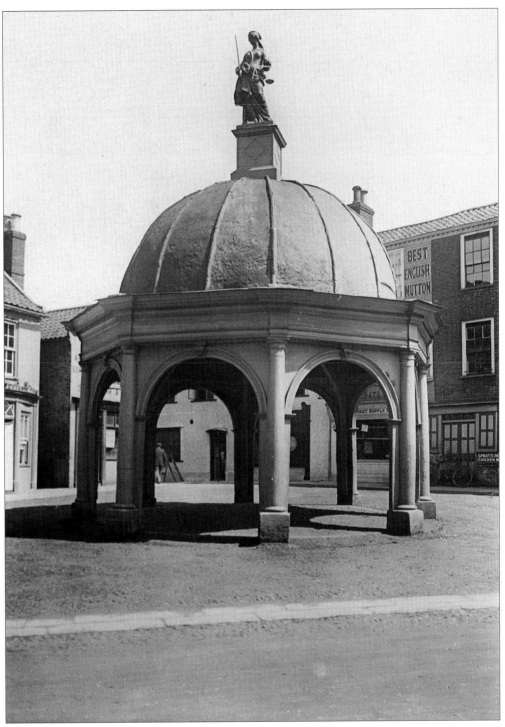

The lead figure of Justice, holding a sword in her right hand and scales in her left, was added to the Butter Cross in 1754. The Direct Meat Supply Company in the shop behind the cross advertises 'Best English Mutton' in an advertisement that has apparently been painted on the wall since the date of the picture on the opposite page.

St Mary's Church, Bungay, is now the town's principal church. This 1920s photograph, reproduced on another of H.W. Short's postcards, shows the then-new town war memorial, bearing the names of 102 Bungay men who died in the First World War. Attached to St Mary's was at one time the church of the Holy Cross, used by the Benedictine nunnery. The nunnery buildings were destroyed in the 1668 fire.

Bridge Street, Bungay, naturally takes its name from the bridge linking Bungay and Ditchingham across the Waveney, which here makes a great loop around Bungay Common. Below is Bungay's second parish church, Holy Trinity, with its eleventh-century round tower.

The big tower mill at Bungay, built in 1830. In the days when windmills ground much of the grain grown on Suffolk farms Bungay had several mills, including a postmill that stood quite close to this one.

Staithe Road which, as its name implies, led to Bungay Staithe, the head of navigation on the Waveney. To reach the staithe, wherries had to negotiate locks at Shipmeadow, Ellingham and Wainford, provided under an Act of Parliament of 1670. The last company to operate the navigation were the local millers and maltsters, W.D. & A.E. Walker, who built some of their own wherries at the staithe. No wherries have come to Bungay since 1934, when the navigation closed.

The wherry *Albion* at Bungay Staithe, *c.* 1900. Although often referred to as 'a Norfolk wherry', the *Albion* was built by Billy Brighton at Oulton Broad and was owned by W.D. & A.E. Walker, so she most definitely belonged to Suffolk.

Skinner's Mill at Stradbroke bore the date 1688 on part of its structure, though it had clearly been rebuilt and updated more than once since its original erection. The patent sails, invented by William Cubitt, who became consulting engineer to Ransomes at Ipswich, and the fantail that kept the mill into wind were nineteenth-century improvements.

The little town of Eye was until local government reorganization in 1974 a self-governing borough with mayor and corporation. Only horse-drawn vehicles are to be seen in this photograph, probably taken *c.* 1912, the youthful driver of the cart in the right foreground being dressed in schoolboy attire of the period. To the left are the shop of John Crisp, saddler, and the Horse Shoes Hotel, whose flaking sign announces it to be a posting establishment. On the opposite side of the street is the shop of Archibald Tipple, boot and shoe maker; Mrs May Tipple, possibly his wife, was about this time recorded as carrying on the trade of stocking knitter.

Schoolchildren, in this case girls, also appear in this photograph of Church Street, Eye, also from the pre-1914 period. The magnificent tower of SS Peter and Paul's Church, which provided a pattern for other parishes to aspire to, dominates the end of the street; wills of the 1450s and 1460s provide evidence of the building activities then going on, and there is a reference to the completion of the tower in 1470. It is said to have been financed 'partly with the plowgh, partly in churchales, partly in legacies given that waye, but chiefly of the frank & devowte hartes of the people'. To the left of the church is the early sixteenth-century Guildhall and on the right is the Eight Bells, kept in the early 1900s by Arthur Read.

In the early nineteenth century the castle hill at Eye was crowned by a post windmill, but this was replaced by the building shown in this view. The shape of the castle bailey laid out by William Malet to the west of the motte can still be seen reflected in the layout of the streets.

THE COAST & HEATHS

Victorian railway builder Samuel Morton Peto, later to be honoured with a baronetcy for his work in constructing a railway in the Crimea to carry supplies to the front, acquired Somerleyton Hall in 1844. On the foundations of the Elizabethan hall he built a Jacobean-style house, and in place of the existing village he built 'cottage-residences of a highly ornamental character' far superior to those occupied by most Victorian workers. His architect was the remarkable John Thomas, whose sculpture adorns the Houses of Parliament.

The main street of Corton, seen above in Edwardian times, bends abruptly to the left at its northern end, though doubtless it once continued on beyond where a cliff marks the present limit of the sea's advance. Much of the Suffolk coast has suffered from erosion, the most spectacular instance being the disappearance of the once-great seaport town of Dunwich which was already battling with the waves in the thirteenth century. Inland lies an area of what was once heathland, known today as the Sandlings. Almost all the heath has been lost to agriculture, to airfields, to forestry or to natural progression, though attempts are being made to save the last remnants by sheep grazing. Natural progression means the progression from heathland to scrubland when birches and thornbushes seed. When the heath was grazed by sheep this kind of vegetation was grazed off and could not get a hold, but without grazing it quite quickly takes over.

There have been coastal lights at Lowestoft since two leading lights were erected in 1609 to bring ships in through the Stanford Channel. The lighthouse seen in this picture of *c.* 1912 was erected in 1873–4 to replace the one built in 1676 at a time when Samuel Pepys was Master of Trinity House.

A series of narrow paths known as scores connect the town of Lowestoft with the Beach, that area of low-lying land below the cliff. In this view of Crown Score *c.* 1910 the Low Light can be seen standing near the water's edge.

A community of fishermen and other seafarers grew up on the Beach during the nineteenth century, and to serve this community Christ Church was built in 1868, two years after a separate ecclesiastical parish had been formed. When this photograph was taken *c.* 1910 as one of a series of postcards for Herbert George Rogers, a newsagent in London Road North, the Beach formed a thriving suburb with its own shops, pubs and institutions; in the 1960s it was cleared to become an industrial estate.

The South Pier which sheltered the outer harbour, built in mid-century by Morton Peto, was also the resort of holidaymakers. This part of Lowestoft became popular after Peto's development of a 'new town' on land south of the bridge, with terraces of brick-built houses designed by sculptor-architect John Thomas. The iron-framed Pier Pavilion seen in this 1890s photograph was opened in 1891 and survived until after the Second World War.

A notice warning that it is dangerous for children to play on the breakwater seems superfluous in these conditions. Seas such as these were responsible for the destruction of Will Edwards'' concert hall on the South Beach on 11 September 1912, as seen below in a photograph by C.T. Metcalf, of London Road South, Lowestoft.

Inland from Lowestoft lies Oulton Broad, the most southerly of what are usually called 'the Norfolk Broads'. When Lowestoft harbour was constructed in the 1830s, as part of a scheme to bring seagoing vessels to Norwich, Oulton Broad and Lake Lothing were separated by a lock; the easterly section of Lake Lothing became the inner harbour, and the lock marked the division between salt water and fresh. The broad is linked with the Waveney by Oulton Dyke, which was widened and deepened to enable seagoing ships to pass through on their way to Norwich and Beccles. Today only pleasure craft are to be seen using the dyke.

To the south of Lowestoft lies the fishing village of Pakefield, a community that has suffered much from attacks by the sea. In between is Kirkley, which merged indefinably into Lowestoft as development proceeded during the nineteenth century and in 1907 became part of the borough of Lowestoft. Almost on the boundary with Pakefield is South Cliff Congregational Church, built at the beginning of this century on land given by James Jeremiah Colman, the mustard manufacturer; the church was quite new when this photograph was taken.

Kessingland was at one time reckoned to be the most prosperous village in Suffolk as a result of its participation in the herring fishing, and some of the beating chambers in which herring nets were repaired can still be seen there. Steam drifters were owned in Kessingland, and indeed the first steam drifter launched in Lowestoft in 1897, the year of Queen Victoria's diamond jubilee, was built for a Kessingland owner, but they worked from Lowestoft harbour. St Edmund's Church, with its lofty fifteenth-century tower, stands as evidence of an earlier prosperity no doubt based on coastal trade and fisheries.

For fifty years, from 1879 to 1929, the narrow-gauge Southwold Railway operated from Halesworth to Southwold. Local legend tells how the rolling stock was brought back from China after the closure of the pioneering Shanghai and Woosung line, but in fact the gauge was different and the Southwold engines were built by Sharp, Stewart in Manchester especially for the Southwold Railway. In fact it was the engine driver who had returned from China, for a Mr W.G. Jackson who had driven the first train on the Woosung tramway became the Southwold Railway's first locomotive foreman. The picture, from the beginning of the century, shows no. 1 *Southwold* in Southwold station.

Fishermen's sheds on the beach at Southwold in the 1880s. In the middle of the picture is a ramshackle shed that shows signs of having been originally roofed with an upturned boat, probably a fishing punt like those lying on the shingle.

A special occasion in Southwold Market Place, *c.* 1909. Unfortunately the reason for the gathering is not known, but it is typical of Southwold that any special event should be attended by such a considerable crowd. The town had a long history of self-government, but the mayor and members of the corporation are not in evidence on this occasion.

St Edmund's Church, Southwold, seen in the late nineteenth century. The church, with its superlative tower, was built in the decades between 1430 and 1460 when the Wars of the Roses were bringing havoc to the kingdom, which perhaps makes the achievement of the builders even more magnificent. Sir Nikolaus Pevsner calls St Edmund's 'the epitome of Suffolk flushwork'.

A photograph from the 1880s of the ferryman who operated the ferry from Southwold to Walberswick sitting in the ferry boat on the Walberswick side. It seems that the ferry was an ancient one, since there is a mention of a ferry boat in the thirteenth century.

In 1885 the River Blyth Ferry Company was formed to provide a chain ferry to carry vehicles across the river, and the original hand-cranked ferry was later replaced by one powered by steam. In this picture from early in the twentieth century a horse-drawn carriage is about to be taken over to Southwold.

Walberswick Church, seen here in a photograph from a Victorian album, fell into decay when the village of Walberswick itself declined in importance and the parishioners became unable to keep such a large building in repair. Most unusually, we do know the names of those responsible for building the fine tower, since in an agreement of 1425 which survives they are named as 'Richard Russel of Dunwich and Adam Powle of Blythburgh'.

The River Blyth was made navigable up to the market town of Halesworth in the 1750s, and for more than a century keels and then wherries fetched by sea from the Broads rivers carried coal and other goods up to the quay seen in the picture above. The Thoroughfare, seen below at a time of celebration in the early years of this century, is the commercial heart of Halesworth.

Henham Hall, the home of the Earls of Stradbroke, was built in 1793 by James Wyatt, twenty years after its Elizabethan predecessor had been destroyed by fire. Edward Barry 'beautified' it in the nineteenth century, but the hall was demolished in 1953. Below is a shoot on the Henham estate in Victorian times.

The town of Dunwich was a thriving seaport in the early Middle Ages, but storms blocked its harbour and submerged its streets, eventually swallowing up almost every building. The last of its eight, or possibly nine, churches to survive the onslaught was All Saints', seen here as a nineteenth-century ruin. A series of picture postcards published this century show it gradually slipping down the cliff as storms ate their way into the land; all is now gone, and the cliff line has reached the western, landward ramparts of the medieval town.

Kelsale lies just to the east of the old Little Yarmouth Turnpike, the main road from Ipswich to Lowestoft and Yarmouth. The guildhall, seen in the 1900-ish picture above, was built in about 1495 and restored in the nineteenth century for use as a parochial school. A couple of miles to the south the main road passed through the middle of Saxmundham, diving under the East Suffolk line railway bridge, seen below *c.* 1920.

Aldeburgh beach and the town's two lifeboats in the early years of the twentieth century. The nearer boat is the no. 1 boat *City of Winchester*, with the no. 2 boat *Edward Z. Dresden* beyond. The former boat was built to replace the ill-fated *Aldeburgh* which capsized on 7 December 1899, with the loss of six of her crew of eighteen. Up to the time of the disaster the *Aldeburgh* had been launched on service fifty-four times, and had saved 152 lives. A later Aldeburgh lifeboat, the motor lifeboat *Abdy Beauclerk*, carried out the first war service of any lifeboat in the British Isles during the Second World War when she went out to the Brocklebank liner *Magdapur* which had been sunk by a magnetic mine just a week after the outbreak of war in 1939.

The former fishing smack *Ionia*, converted to a houseboat, was a feature of the River Alde at Aldeburgh for more than half a century. A fleet of cod smacks once worked out of Aldeburgh, but the *Ionia* was not one of them; she had been a Grimsby trawling smack working from the Humber.

Opposite. Snape windmill, which was dismantled in the 1930s. The brick roundhouse was converted into a house and was used by Benjamin Britten when composing some of his music.

Framlingham is a small town that owed its early importance to the castle established by Roger Bigod on land given to him *c.* 1100 by Henry I. In later days 'Fram' was the centre of an agricultural area well known for dairying. Gostling & Company had this chemist's shop on the Market Hill at Framlingham at the beginning of this century, and from the evidence of the bills on display in the photograph they were much involved in veterinary medicines. Herbert Sara seems to have taken over the business *c.* 1914.

A flourishing port on the River Deben, Woodbridge was in the nineteenth century a busy place with many maltings, mills, a shipyard and an iron foundry. The junction of Cumberland Street, to the left in the above picture, the Thoroughfare, to the right, and Church Street, straight ahead, is known as Cross Corner, from The Cross public house, said on the sign to have been established in 1652; the public house probably took its name from the crossroads in the first place. The photographer is unknown, but the postcard was published by George Booth, printer and stationer in Church Street. At the mouth of the Deben is Felixstowe Ferry, seen in the picture below looking across the river to Bawdsey.

Prominent in this photograph of Felixstowe beach, taken in the summer of 1889, is Charles Emeny's photographic studio. Charles Emeny and his son Clement chronicled the development of the town, which became a popular resort after the Empress of Germany, a daughter of Queen Victoria, chose to bring her

family to the town for a seaside holiday in 1891 while the Emperor was carrying out his official duties on a visit to Britain. The tower of South Beach Mansion, where the Empress stayed, can be seen above the row of buildings in the right background. (David Cleveland)

Among the Victorian businessmen from Ipswich who acquired summer homes in Felixstowe and Walton, the older settlement lying just inland from the new resort, was Richard Dykes Alexander. This early photograph, probably taken by Alexander himself, shows the Alexanders at Lavender Cottage, Walton, in the 1860s. So long was the usual exposure that it was possible for the photographer to put himself in the picture. (Suffolk Record Office)

IPSWICH & AROUND

At the bottom of Bourne Hill, on the approach to Ipswich from the Manningtree direction, stands the Wherstead Ostrich, a hostelry that is said to have been built in 1612. The sign of the Ostrich, a bird of that kind with a horseshoe in its beak, was taken from the crest of Sir Edward Coke, the seventeenth-century Chief Justice, who acquired the manor of Bourne Hall, on whose lands the inn was built, in 1609. In 1996 the name was changed to The Oyster Reach, lending credence to an historical misapprehension that attributed the name to nearby oyster layings in the Orwell. (Hugh Moffat)

Pond Hall Farm on the Ipswich side of the Orwell some distance below the town, seen *c.* 1900 in a photograph taken by Alexander Moffat, an amateur photographer who became town clerk of Ipswich. The photograph of the Ostrich on the previous page was also taken by him. Near Pond Hall at John's Ness the Ipswich shipbuilder John Barnard built the Fourth Rate *Hampshire* of fifty guns in 1741. (Hugh Moffat)

Almost opposite Pond Hall stands Freston Tower, an enigmatic Tudor tower in diapered red brickwork standing in parkland sloping up from the river, here seen in a photograph from a Victorian album. Tradition associates the tower with the Latimers, but it was probably built by a prominent Ipswich merchant, Thomas Gooding, who succeeded the Latimers at Freston. There are many legends connected with the tower, but they are just that, legends.

Gainsborough Lane, on the eastern outskirts of Ipswich, was a favourite with photographers and postcard publishers at the beginning of the twentieth century. Today the land is covered with council houses. In the picture below harvesters are at work in the field not many miles from the centre of Ipswich.

As the town expanded houses were built on the town rampart surrounding the medieval core of Ipswich. These houses in Tower Ramparts survived well into this century, but both the houses and the rampart have disappeared since the photograph was taken.

Above is Upper Brook Street, Ipswich, *c.* 1885, with the shops at the end of the Buttermarket projecting
in the background. The road was widened there in the 1930s. In the Buttermarket is the Ancient House,
seen on the opposite page in the 1890s when Fred Pawsey was occupying it as a bookshop and stationer. It
is apparent that even a hundred years ago tourists were coming to Ipswich, to judge from the
advertisement in the window. The pargeting on the walls of the Ancient House dates from *c.* 1670,
whereas the house itself is older.

Richard Dykes Alexander took this photograph of the cottage occupied by 'the keeper of the Promenade' in the 1860s. The Promenade was an avenue alongside the New Cut which used to be a favourite resort of Ipswich people, and the cottage stood roughly where the entrance to the Wet Dock is now. (Suffolk Record Office)

Another early photograph by Richard Dykes Alexander shows the Umbrella shelter at the end of the Promenade. Although the Promenade was lost to Ipswich as a result of dock expansion between the two world wars the Umbrella survived in a state of increasing dilapidation into the 1950s. (Suffolk Record Office)

When the Ipswich Ragged School attempted in 1849 to provide some kind of education for children 'too ragged, too filthy, too ignorant, for ordinary instruction' it was Richard Dykes Alexander who provided the money to pay for the school's operations. The children were taught to be self-sufficient, and to that end (in this photograph by Alexander) the master, Joshua Newman, is superintending them in cutting and bundling firewood. No doubt the sales of the bundles helped to pay for the day-to-day work of the school. (Suffolk Record Office)

Robert Burrows, an Ipswich artist turned photographer, took this photograph of a barquentine at Ipswich in 1858. He seems to have had a particular interest in the local shipping, for he took many pictures in and around the Wet Dock, which when opened in 1842 was the biggest of its kind in the country, much larger than any dock on the Thames or at Hull or Liverpool. (Suffolk Record Office)

Overleaf. The Ipswich Lifeboat Saturday procession passing over Cornhill on 10 July 1897, taken by Alexander Moffat. The background to the picture is provided by T.W. Cotman's distinctive façade of 1889. (Hugh Moffat)

Looking west along Tavern Street in the 1880s. Prominent on the right of this photograph by William Vick are the premises of Lewis Brothers, linen drapers and silk mercers, who declared in an advertisement that their black silks 'have been sent to all parts of England, Scotland, to the Continent of Europe, and to the English Colonies'. By the 1890s the Lewises had been succeeded by Sydney William Cook, who carried on the same trade for several more years before the premises were taken over by the Capital & Counties Bank.

In 1867 the old town hall was replaced by an imposing building 'in the Venetian style', which was in 1881 joined by an almost equally imposing head post office. Cornhill had, as its name suggests, originally been the site of the corn market, and it was for many years until 1812 used for the sale of cattle. At one side of Cornhill stood St Mildred's Church, which became redundant in the Middle Ages and was converted into a town hall; the last traces of the former church were removed when the old town hall was demolished for the building of the new. In the same way the Corn Exchange which had in 1812 taken the place of a strange building called the Rotunda itself gave way to the new post office building in 1880–1, a new Corn Exchange then being erected behind the town hall.

As the town expanded during the nineteenth century many Ipswich landmarks disappeared. One of them was the Brook's Hall pond, seen here in a photograph of 1869, another of those issued by William Vick although it is possible it was taken by his predecessor William Cobb. The pond was filled in when houses spread along Norwich Road. Note the loose surface of what was then the main road to Stowmarket, Bury St Edmunds and Norwich.

CENTRAL SUFFOLK

Encapsulated within Sir Charles Barry's Italianate mansion at Shrubland, 5 miles north of Ipswich, is the eighteenth-century hall built by James Paine for the Rev. John Bacon. The gardens were modelled by Barry on those of the Villa d'Este at Tivoli. Today Shrubland attracts those who can afford to seek their health expensively and looks down on the roaring traffic of the A14 trunk road.

Sir Charles Barry's gardens were altered later in the nineteenth century by William Robinson, creator of the English herbaceous border. Coddenham Lodge, below, on the eastern side of Shrubland Park, still appears to have been transplanted from Tuscany.

The unusual weatherboarded top stage of the tower distinguishes the church of St Mary and St Lambert, Stonham Aspal. It was added in the eighteenth century by Squire Theodore Eccleston, who was so keen a bellringer that he substituted a ring of ten for the original five bells and needed an extra-large bell chamber to house them. The Bullnose Morris bears an East Sussex registration; did it perhaps belong to the unknown photographer? In the churchyard is a monument to the Revd Anthony Wingfield which, says Sir Nikolaus Pevsner, 'is so unlike anything one is used to in churchyards that one feels a monument in Westminster Abbey may be taking a country holiday'.

The Magpie at Stonham Parva, known to travellers of a bygone age as 'Stonham Pie', once had a live magpie in the cage to be seen on the front wall beside the door. It also possessed a sign spanning the Norwich road, a Roman road known as the Pye Road from which it got its name. In spite of the great increase in traffic it still retains its sign across the road, but the cage no longer contains a live bird.

Every Suffolk town has its story of disaster by fire, some being almost totally destroyed as the flames leapt from building to building and street to street, fanned by a fresh breeze. It was on a Sunday morning in July 1868 that fire broke out in Bury Street, Stowmarket, and no fewer than eighty-one people were made homeless. (Ivan Codd)

Although in the nineteenth century Stowmarket became a minor industrial centre with an agricultural engineering works and foundry, an artificial fertilizer factory and even an explosives works, it continued to play its traditional role as a market town midway between Ipswich and Bury St Edmunds. This view of the market, held in the triangular Market Place, dates from the early 1920s; later in the decade Samuel Pluck's outfitter's shop and boot store became the National Provincial Bank, and Pluck retreated to his other store in Station Road. (Ivan Codd)

Overleaf. All over the country people celebrated Queen Victoria's Diamond Jubilee in 1897. Here the crowds gather in the Market Place at Stowmarket for the celebrations, with the men of Combs Brass Band in their smart uniforms ready to provide music for the occasion. (Ivan Codd)

For a few years just before the outbreak of the First World War Charles Miller had a hardware store in Regent Street, Stowmarket, and a horse-drawn cart in which he hawked his wares around the surrounding villages. Along with his pots and pans he sold woven wire covers to keep the flies off the cold joint, and also Lipton's tea. Many small communities depended on such traders for household articles, for a trip to the nearest market town was by no means an everyday occurrence. (Ivan Codd)

A view of Ipswich Street, Stowmarket, in the early years of this century, with the Duke's Head on the left and the tower and spire of the parish church of St Peter and St Mary looming in the background. Until the construction of the Gipping Valley bypass in quite recent years this was part of the main road between Ipswich, Bury St Edmunds and Cambridge, yet traffic is so slight that youngsters have no fears about posing in the middle of the street for the photographer. The Duke's Head still exists, but the rest of the scene has changed dramatically as the result of redevelopment. (Ivan Codd)

The Prentice family began producing artificial manure at Stowmarket in 1856, and in the following decade branched out into the manufacture of guncotton. The manufacturing process was far from safe, and in 1864 two women employees died in an explosion; a much more devastating series of explosions occurred in 1871, resulting in the deaths of twenty-four people and widespread damage to the town. Above is a view of the rebuilt works on the River Gipping, *c.* 1900. (Ivan Codd)

A march undertaken by strikers from the explosives works during a long-lasting dispute with the New Explosives Company in 1913; they are making their way along Ipswich Street. In spite of increasing hardship in the town the strikers held out for an increase in local wages that were below those paid in the industry elsewhere. (Ivan Codd)

Overleaf. The absence of traffic is noticeable in this view of Bury Street, Stowmarket, looking up from the Tavern Street junction. The juxtaposition of William Huble Druce's haircutting, shaving and shampooing establishment and the cycle shop of T.H. Nice & Company, with its Michelin advertisements, dates the photograph to *c.* 1906. (Ivan Codd)

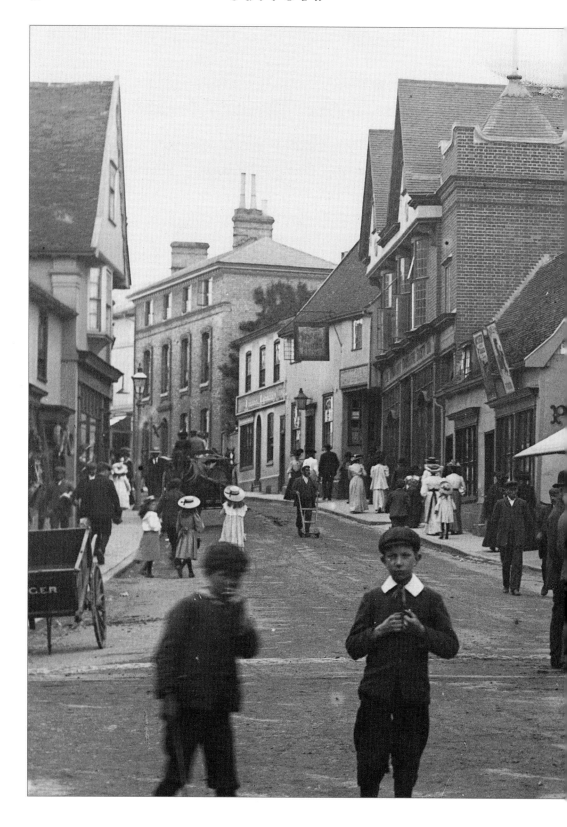

Travelling showmen had their fixed times for visiting different places, often based on the dates of the old trading or hiring fairs of earlier centuries. At Stowmarket they were still using the Dukes Head Meadow in Temple Road, off Ipswich Street, in the 1920s, by which time motor caravans were taking over from the traditional horse-drawn caravans of earlier days. The Regal cinema was built on the site in 1936 and the showmen had to find another setting for the fair. (Ivan Codd)

Opposite. The Deanery Tower at Hadleigh, completed *c.* 1495, was built by William Pykenham, Archdeacon of Suffolk, who was appointed rector of Hadleigh in 1472. It is generally supposed that the tower was to have been the gatehouse to a palace whose building was brought to an end by Pykenham's death in 1497. Besides being a fine example of fifteenth-century brickwork the Deanery Tower has its place in ecclesiastical history as the setting for a conference in 1833 which gave rise to the Oxford Movement.

Two views of Hadleigh High Street in the days when traffic was horse drawn and was limited to the occasional waggon or cart. On the right of the picture above can be seen the Coffee Tavern at 66 High Street, established *c.* 1890 in an attempt to break the attraction of the public houses; it was in being for around half a century, and the name is still used for the end shop of this seventeenth-century block. The lower picture, looking in the opposite direction, shows the White Lion Hotel and a building with a pargetted upper storey which fortunately survives. In both pictures it is possible to see water running in the deep gutters; in spite of a petition presented to the Local Board in 1881 by High Street residents complaining of 'the stench which arises from this gutter in consequence of its being used as a drain', the water continued to run until well within living memory.

The original part of Hadleigh Guildhall, the central double-jettied section in this view, dates back to the mid-fifteenth century when it served as a market house. The market rights were granted to the lord of the manor of Toppesfield Manor in 1252 and were transferred by William de Clopton to fifteen trustees in 1438; the successors to those trustees, the Hadleigh Market Feoffment, still operate the Guildhall and have in recent years spent a large amount on its restoration. The building has in its time been used as a school, as a workhouse and as the town hall, a new town hall being built on to the old Guildhall in the nineteenth century.

The village of Brettenham lies some 7 miles to the west of Stowmarket. The little River Brett rises in the parish and makes its way through Chelsworth and Hadleigh to its confluence with the Stour near Higham. The name of the village is thought to be derived from Bretta's ham or home, Bretta possibly being 'the Briton'; the river name is a back-formation from the village. In about 1830 Joseph Bonaparte, brother of Napoleon and ex-king of Naples and of Spain, lived at Brettenham Hall, which in later years when it was the residence of Sir Thomas Courtenay Theydon Warner MP was surrounded by somewhat fabulous gardens. The hall is now a school.

THE STOUR VALLEY

The lower part of the Stour is well known as Constable Country, while the upper section towards Sudbury is forever linked with Thomas Gainsborough, who was the son of a Sudbury weaver. John Constable's father operated Flatford Mill and young John learned his trade as a miller. All the elements that John said made him an artist are seen in this view of Flatford taken on a glass plate negative by an unknown turn-of-the-century photographer.

John Constable produced a number of sketches and paintings of St Mary's Church in his native village of East Bergholt. This photograph, printed from a glass plate exposed by an unknown photographer *c.* 1900, shows the church very much as the artist knew it, though the interior was considerably altered by the Victorians. An early Constable drawing shows the chancel interior with a substantial gallery spanning the chancel arch and box pews almost hiding the Laudian altar rails, replaced later by telescopic brass rails.

The tower of East Bergholt church was never completed because the Reformation brought an end to bequests to such building projects, so the ring of bells is in a bell cage in the churchyard. Instead of being operated by bell-ropes from below the bells have to be swung by hand by ringers standing on the bell frame.

A view of Flatford Mill, once operated by John Constable's father, Golding Constable, seen from the Essex side of the river. Flour produced at the mill was taken downstream by lighters and transhipped at Mistley Quay into seagoing vessels, including Golding Constable's *Telegraph*, for onward carriage to London. Just above the mill was a dry dock in which the river lighters were built and repaired, as seen in Constable's sketch of boatbuilding, Flatford, dated 7 September 1814, and the painting exhibited at the Royal Academy the following year.

Dedham Vale is known as the Constable Country, and to those who know his pictures well reminders of the artist are everywhere to be seen. This picture of Stoke-by-Nayland Church, printed from a glass plate negative of *c*. 1900, shows a scene almost identical to that sketched by Constable in 1814, except that the little building on the left does not appear in the drawing.

Edward Baker's mills at Great Cornard were originally powered only by the water of the River Stour, which also served to carry the flour they produced on its way to London. The arrival of steam power enabled Baker to expand his mills, and towards the end of the nineteenth century the old millstones were replaced by roller mills introduced by Suffolk millwrights from eastern Europe.

At the beginning of the twentieth century the village of Great Cornard, on the Suffolk side of the Stour
little more than a mile from Sudbury, had a population of fewer than a thousand. The scattered village
whose centre is seen in the photograph above has been expanded since the Second World War by the
building of large estates by the Greater London Council to house those who sought to escape from the
Metropolis.

The tower of All Saints' Church, Sudbury, is prominent in this view across the old timber Ballingdon Bridge in the early years of this century. Sudbury is a very ancient town with a history of cloth manufacture; although production of woollen cloth ceased many years ago it still has several silk mills. The timber bridge seen here was later replaced by a new bridge in more modern materials. (John Wilton)

There is a story that bull baiting used to be one of the attractions at the Bull Inn, Sudbury, seen here with the tower of All Saints' Church looming over it. The building dates from the middle of the sixteenth century and the main door, made of oak plank, used to have the date 1694 scratched on it. It is no longer a public house, having lost its licence in the 1950s.

Stour Street contains fine timber-framed houses and was once inhabited by some of the town's more affluent residents. In the picture above we are looking out of town towards Cross Street, and in the one below we are looking back towards Gainsborough Street, on the corner of which are the premises of Ebenezer Hitchcock, cooper (a maker of barrels); on the wall he advertises also 'creamery and dairy', so it seems that like many old-time tradesmen he had several strings to his bow.

Cross Street is one of Sudbury's oldest streets, described by Celia Fiennes in 1689 as an 'aristocratic suburb'. On the right is a fifteenth-century house long known as 'Ye Old Moot Hall'; the Moot Hall was in fact on the Market Hill, but this building might at one time have been a guildhall. In the 1890s a woman photographer, Miss Susanna Berry, was working from 78 Cross Street. Since this photograph was taken, *c.* 1912, some of the buildings have been cleared away and replaced; indeed after the Second World War a report recommended the eradication of the whole area, which had gained a poor reputation, but wiser counsels have since prevailed.

On 1 October 1929 the civic pride of the Borough of Sudbury is blossoming, and hundreds throng Market Hill to watch the proceedings. The United States Ambassador, General Charles Gates Dawes, whose ancestor William Dawes sailed in the ship *Planter* to settle in the New World, is to be admitted an Honorary Freeman of the borough. In the picture opposite the mayor, Edward Page FitzGerald, presents General Dawes with an illuminated scroll recording the council's resolution to grant him the honorary freedom. (East Anglian Film Archive)

Today, in spite of the opening of a bypass, traffic pours through Long Melford's main street in an almost continuous stream. In this view of Hall Street at the beginning of the century there is no sign of any traffic whatever, unless one includes cattle only loosely controlled by a boy with a stout stick. Are they perhaps heading for the slaughterhouse behind Alfred Allen's butcher's shop on the right-hand side, with its blind extended to keep the sun off the meat?

The photographer's bicycle leans against a lamp post, his heavy leather case strapped to the carrier, while he sets up this shot of Melford Green, with Holy Trinity Church and Trinity Hospital at the head of the green. The church is one of the finest in Suffolk, but the tower which seems to complement the building so well is, surprisingly, a modern rebuilding. The original was lost in a fire, and the replacement built early in the eighteenth century was somewhat lacking in stature; it was 'restored' by George F. Bodley between 1900 and 1904 to match the scale and character of the rest of the church, the new tower encasing the eighteenth-century one.

The photographer's bicycle appears again in this picture of the gate to Melford Hall, home of the Hyde Parker family. Before the Dissolution of the Monasteries the hall belonged to the abbots of Bury St Edmunds, and some time in the middle of the sixteenth century it was acquired from Henry VIII by lawyer Sir William Cordell, one of those people who was able to survive changes of monarch and of religion in that difficult period. In 1578 his fortune, made through his legal career, was put to the test when he entertained Queen Elizabeth I at Melford. We are told that 'there was in Suffolke suche sumptuous feastinges and bankets as seldom in anie parte of the worlde there hath been seene afore. The Maister of the Rolles, Sir William Cordell, was the first that bganne this greate feastinge at his house of Melforde, and did lyght such a candle to the rest of the shire, that they were gladd bountifullie and francklie to followe the same example.' Some fortunes were consumed in the flame of that candle, but not Sir William's.

The name Melford is said to be derived from the mill ford. In this photograph the site of the ford can be seen as well as the weatherboarded building of the Hall Mill, one of three corn mills that once existed in Long Melford. In the foreground is one of the gas lamps supplied by the local gasworks, at one time owned by the local ironfounders, Ward & Silver, and later by the Long Melford Gas Co. Ltd.

Lavenham is visited by thousands of tourists every year because it has retained so many of its fine timber-framed buildings, but it is by no means as unchanging as many of the visitors imagine. Above is a photograph taken by F. Lingard Ranson, Lavenham photographer and historian, of the old post office on the corner of High Street and Hall Lane, probably just before or just after the First World War. The next-door building, now known as The Crooked House, has a nineteenth-century frontage to the ground floor; in the later picture on the opposite page the nineteenth-century brickwork and sash windows have been replaced by a timber-framed wall with leaded windows in the position of the Tudor original.

The well-known Swan Hotel at Lavenham, standing at the junction of High Street and Water Street (so called from the stream which still flows beneath ground), was at one time a coaching inn. The old coach entrance can be seen in this view beneath a large sign advertising Ward's Champion ales and stouts, brewed just across the Essex boundary at Foxearth. Later the old entrance was stopped up and the plaster was stripped away from the walls to reveal the timbering, giving the building a very different appearance.

BURY ST EDMUNDS

Bury St Edmunds largely owes its existence to the Benedictine monastery whose remains are still to be seen between the town and the River Lark. The precinct wall of the abbey is carried across the river on a twelfth-century bridge that has been the subject of generations of photographers. The body of King Edmund, who was probably killed by the Danes a few miles to the south at Bradfield St Clare rather than at the other sites mentioned by tradition, was brought to the abbey after his martyrdom in 869. His shrine attracted pilgrims both poor and rich in great numbers during the Middle Ages.

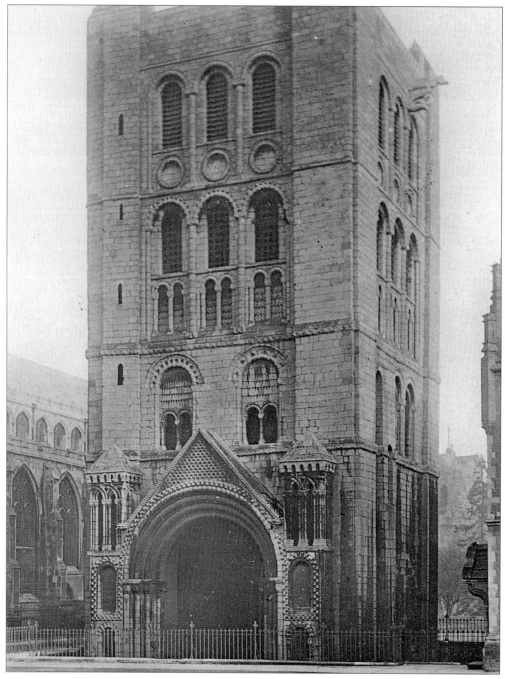

The Norman Gate was built under Abbot Anselm in the first half of the twelfth century to provide an entrance gate to the abbey church, an enormous building 50 ft longer than Norwich Cathedral. The relatively ornate decoration of the side facing the town made the gate, seen here at the beginning of the twentieth century after it had lost its battlements, a splendid entry for those on pilgrimage to the shrine of St Edmund who included royalty as well as the common people. After the destruction of the abbey the tower served as a campanile or bell tower for St James's Church, which in 1914 became the Cathedral of the new Diocese of St Edmundsbury and Ipswich.

A portrait of Sarah Fennell taken by Clarke & Wallace, of 28 Angel Hill, Bury St Edmunds, in May 1866 when she was aged ninety-one. Sarah, a member of the Society of Friends, left money to another member who used it to build four flats on land sold to her by the Bury Monthly Meeting. The intention was that the flats should be made available to 'respectable women in reduced circumstances, but with some income of their own, able and willing to read the Bible to the poor of Bury and to engage in other home-mission work as required'. The building in St Andrew's Street was probably the first purpose-built block of flats in the town.

Bury St Edmunds station is a somewhat imposing building that was still incomplete when first brought into use towards the end of 1847. It is seen here *c.* 1900, by which time the trainshed roof between the

two towers had been removed. Prominent in this view are the horse buses which met trains and took passengers to hotels in the town. (Suffolk Record Office)

King Edward VII and Queen Alexandra visited Bury St Edmunds on 17 December 1904, their visit being recorded by the local photographers whose pictures were hastily published as postcards. Above, the King is seen leaving St James's Church, and below his carriage, escorted by members of the Duke of York's (Loyal Suffolk Hussars) Suffolk Imperial Yeomanry, is turning from Angel Hill into Abbeygate Street. (John Wilton)

Little more than a month before the royal visit General Lord Methuen had unveiled a memorial to Suffolk men who had fallen in the South African War. By a strange coincidence the ceremony took place on 11 November, which was later to become Remembrance Day. The troops in light grey uniforms on the left are the Volunteers, members of the 2nd Volunteer Battalion, Suffolk Regiment; eight companies were based in Bury, with their headquarters at the Old Militia Barracks in Cemetery Road. Close by the memorial are a half-dozen newspaper reporters taking down Lord Methuen's speech. (John Wilton)

The corporation water cart on the left of this picture of Bury Market Place is sprinkling water to lay the dust. This is probably the Wednesday market, pictured *c.* 1908; the Saturday provision market filled the entire square. On the left, beyond the water cart, is Moyse's Hall, a stone-built house dating from the later twelfth century and traditionally said to have been originally the home of a Jew; there is no historical evidence to support this tradition. For many years it served as the Bridewell and the borough police station, but in 1899 it was opened as a museum. (John Wilton)

The Town Hall in Cornhill, seen in a frame from a ciné film made in Bury St Edmunds in 1913. Built on the site of the old Market Cross, destroyed with much of the town in a disastrous fire in 1608, it was used as a playhouse in which the Duke of Grafton's Comedians performed 'Bury Fair' in 1734. It was rebuilt in 1774 to the designs of Robert Adam. (East Anglian Film Archive)

Smith & Sons' shop at 37 and 38 Cornhill is prominent in the above view of Bury market some time before the First World War. A fine new street lamp has been erected, but in the photograph below taken in the 1920s the lamp post appears to be lightless. (John Wilton)

Abbeygate Street, Bury St Edmunds, in the 1920s, looking towards the Abbey Gate. Motor traffic has made its appearance, but there is still space enough for the errand boy to lean on his bicycle outside the outfitter's shop of Sidney Lodge (formerly Thomas Crick's) to watch the antics of the photographer. 'One looks over and across to The Mount (just under a mile away), yet with the feeling that but one stride and the romantic would have one foot in the heart of the town and the other among the trees in the country which surrounds it,' says Harry Marsh, a former mayor of Bury. 'A Ministry order has preserved this view for all time to the great disappointment of the "planners",' he adds.

The tradesmen of Bury as well as the townspeople generally turned out in force for the Lifeboat Saturday procession around the town in July 1906. The procession ended in the Lower Abbey Gardens, where these photographs were taken by one of the local photographers, who rapidly issued a set of postcards portraying the various floats. A pulling and sailing lifeboat on its launching carriage, which can just be seen in the lower picture on the opposite page, took part in the event. A pulling and sailing lifeboat is one that is dependent on oars and sail for propulsion, as opposed to a modern motor lifeboat. (John Wilton)

This pole waggon, a vehicle normally used for the transport of timber, has been used to accommodate one of the trade displays. Those staffing the float, who all seem to be dressed in their Sunday best under their carpenters' aprons, wear the folded paper hats traditionally worn by carpenters. To the left of the upper picture can be glimpsed the float of Robert Williams, saddler of Brentgovel Street, Bury, seen in its entirety below. (John Wilton)

One of the gems of Bury St Edmunds is the Theatre Royal, built in 1819 to the designs of the younger William Wilkins, son of the William Wilkins who had in 1799 obtained the lease of the theatres at Norwich, Colchester, Bury and Yarmouth. Its construction was financed by £100 subscriptions which entitled the subscriber to a silver ticket qualifying him to attend any performance he liked for the rest of his life as well as 5 per cent interest on his shares. After languishing for years as a barrel store for the local brewers the theatre was restored to its original use. Apart from being the only provincial Regency theatre surviving in its original structural form, it is remembered as the theatre that hosted the première of Brandon Thomas's play *Charley's Aunt*; the advertising card opposite reflects its long-running popularity. (John Wilton)

After the First World War a number of the original tanks were presented to various towns as war relics or memorials. This one in the Abbey Gardens at Bury is seen in a postcard sent home in 1923 to a farmer's wife at Newbourne, near Woodbridge, by her young brother who had just enlisted in the Suffolk Regiment at Bury's Gibraltar Barracks. 'Sorry I have not written before,' he writes, 'but we got our equipment and I have been busy cleaning it up.' In his years of service, which took him to the Far East and to China, he no doubt spent many hours polishing and blancoing his equipment. The first tanks were sent to a training camp at Elveden, about ten miles north of Bury, where crews and machines were put through their paces before being sent to France. (Mrs Marion Leeson)

THE LARK & LITTLE OUSE

The River Lark was made navigable to Bury St Edmunds so that coal and other goods could be brought upriver from the port of King's Lynn. On the river lies Mildenhall, whose Market Cross is seen here in a photograph taken in about 1910. At left can be seen the shop of Harry F. Ungless, fancy draper, which after his death in 1906 was run by Mrs Ungless, who was a milliner. Lying near the edge of the Fens, Mildenhall is the largest parish in Suffolk and contains a number of outlying hamlets. A probable reason for the parish being so extensive is that much of the land was marginal and a large area was needed to support the population.

The red-brick Tudor gatehouse of West Stow Hall, near where the Icknield Way crosses the River Lark, with its octagonal corner turrets bearing the arms of Henry VIII's sister Mary Tudor, Queen of France and Duchess of Suffolk, who is buried in St Mary's Church at Bury St Edmunds. At the time this photograph was taken in the 1890s the hall was the home of Henry Frost, Earl Cadogan's agent. (Mrs M. Leeson)

Looking across the Market Place at Mildenhall in the 1920s, with the cycle shop of D. Cattermole, formerly Mrs Mabel Kemp's and earlier William Kemp's, on the right. The premises of a saddler and harnessmaker, Isaac Minns, is just beyond. Dominating the background is the fifteenth-century tower of St Mary's Church.

Mildenhall parish church is one of the great churches of Suffolk, with a magnificent roof whose angels bear the marks of shot supposedly fired at them by Puritan soldiers. The tracery of the east window, well seen in this view, is somewhat remarkable, and the mighty tower, completed by 1464, is a landmark for miles around; until 1831 it was capped by a lantern and spirelet, which would have given it an even more impressive appearance.

Mildenhall High Street *c.* 1910, with the Tiger's Head and the shop of Henry Matthew Burt, bookseller, stationer and printer, on the right. It is quite possible that this and other views in the same series were taken by a visiting photographer and reproduced as postcards for sale in Burt's shop. There were several firms which were in the business of producing postcards for such local shops.

A view of High Street and the church tower from the Market Place taken in the 1930s. The imposing house seen in the photograph on page 133 has been turned into a pair of shops, the right-hand one of which is run by Henry Montague Stiles, outfitter; the other, named Lucille, was run by the Misses N. and P. Sewell. The building on the left, seen also in the previous illustration, has had the plaster stripped off to reveal the timbering and has become Barclays Bank.

The deep gutters in Mill Street, Mildenhall, are bridged by cast-iron channels outside each door in this 1920s view, looking towards High Street. The car parked by the edge of the road bears an early West Suffolk registration, CF-3131 (note the hyphen).

The Lark enters the Great Ouse between Prickwillow and Littleport, and the Little Ouse has its confluence with the major river a few miles downstream at Brandon Creek. Barges could travel up the Little Ouse to Brandon and Thetford through a number of staunches like the one at Brandon, above. In the picture below of Brandon bridge two sunken lighters provide a foreground feature for the photographer. (John Wilton)

These Edwardian youngsters fishing from the old bridge at Brandon, or watching others fishing, attracted Jarrolds' photographer as he travelled round seeking subjects for his firm's postcards. Old warehouses and maltings beside the river provide evidence of a waterborne trade that had already come to an end.

IN THE WEST

Haverhill had a population of little more than 3,000 in the nineteenth century, yet it was a thriving town whose main employers, Gurteen & Sons, had a workforce of more than 2,500 in 1879. This view of the junction of Wratting Road and Withersfield Road in the 1890s shows the premises of James Henderson, ropemaker, and on the right the Rose and Crown Hotel. In the foreground is a two-horse coal cart belonging to the Haverhill Industrial Co-operative Society. (Haverhill & District Local History Group)

Haverhill High Street in 1868, with the Bell Hotel in the middle of the picture and Gurteen's office next-door. The buildings on the left were in the churchyard. The shop on the extreme right became the Coffee Tavern in 1880, as can be seen in the picture on the opposite page. (Haverhill & District Local History Group)

Looking the other way along Haverhill High Street in the 1880s, with The Anchor Coffee Tavern and Dining Rooms, otherwise known as the Coffee Tavern for short, on the left in rather uncomfortable proximity to the yard occupied by Greene & Son, the Bury St Edmunds brewers. The Temperance movement inaugurated coffee taverns and similar establishments in many towns in an endeavour to attract working men away from the public houses. On the right are Chauntry House, then the residence of the senior Daniel Gurteen, and Market Hill Chapel, which is now a shop. The photographer is not recorded, but the picture was issued by Chevens & Son, printers of 25 High Street, as were others of the town at this period. (Haverhill & District Local History Group)

Haverhill High Street towards the end of the nineteenth century, with the 1889 Corn Exchange on the left
(labelled 'Furniture Warehouse'). The horse van belongs to William Byford, who besides being a corn

and coal merchant operated as a carrier between the town and the local railway stations. (Haverhill & District Local History Group)

This photograph of Haverhill Brass Band was taken in 1889 by local photographer Charles Mizon, who was himself a band member. At the time of this photograph they were wearing military-style helmets with brass spikes, but an earlier photograph shows the bandsmen, including Mizon, wearing soft-topped peaked caps. (Haverhill & District Local History Group)

There were three windmills in Haverhill, the best remembered being the big mid-nineteenth-century tower mill that stood to the north of the town until its demolition in 1942. The miller, Richard Ruffle, designed his own annular sail which was some 50 ft in diameter with 120 5-ft vanes, basing it on the invention of an Essex miller, Henry Chopping. This mill worked until 1933, when it suffered damage which put it out of action.

Only St Mary's Church survives of the buildings shown on this photograph of Peas Hill, Haverhill, issued in the 1880s by Chevens & Son. The bystanders have all been warned to remain still while the exposure is taken; it is remarkable that not one face is blurred. (Haverhill & District Local History Group)

The Haverhill celebrations of Queen Victoria's Diamond Jubilee in 1897 photographed by George Moss, who succeeded Charles Mizon as the local photographer during the mid-1890s. A variety of fancy dress is worn by the cyclists in the foreground. The significance of Daniel Maynard Gurteen being dressed as a pig in a smock is forgotten, but the smock would have been one of those made by his family firm. (Haverhill & District Local History Group)

Haverhill's younger generation gathers as the photographer sets up his camera on its tripod in the middle of High Street one day in the 1890s. Few of them heeded his warning to keep still, and the picture is somewhat marred by the many blurs that have resulted. The east end of St Mary's Church can be seen in the distance beyond Chauntry House; on the right is the Red Lion, supplied by P.L. Hudson's brewery at Pampisford in Cambridgeshire. The solitary street light was one of those lit by gas from the gasworks set up in 1854 and acquired by the local authority in 1886. (Haverhill & District Local History Group)

Spring cleaning in Edwardian Haverhill: carpets from The Mount, to which Daniel Maynard Gurteen had moved from Chauntry House, are being cleaned on the tennis lawn by, it is thought, William Webb, Freddie Ford, Bill Reede and Freddie Ford's father. In the background can be seen the Old Independent Congregational Church, which was attended by the Gurteen family. (Haverhill & District Local History Group)

Haverhill Brass Band sets off at 2 p.m. from outside the Old Rectory, later known as Anne of Cleves House, at the head of the procession organized to celebrate the Coronation of King George V in 1911. The celebrations had started in the morning with the ringing of church bells and firing of guns, the ceremonial signing of a loyal address by the urban district council and a thanksgiving service in St Mary's Church. This and the following photographs were almost certainly taken by a member of the Gurteen family and were given to the Haverhill & District Local History Group by Miss Grace Gurteen. (Haverhill & District Local History Group)

One section of the coronation procession was for ladies in period costume; entrants are seen on the right setting off along Hamlet Road. (Haverhill & District Local History Group)

This entry, on a wagon owned by Gurteen & Son, was a group of 'Druids'. The costumes had been used two years earlier in a pageant of religious history presented by the Haverhill and District Sunday School Union. (Haverhill & District Local History Group)

Haverhill Fire Brigade, whose fire station was in Duddery Road, are seen here outside the Old Rectory with their manual fire engine as they take part in the coronation procession; they won first prize in their section. (Haverhill & District Local History Group)

Celia Smart, Grace Gurteen and Joyce Boardman in their Cinderella costumes in the Gurteen family's car, which had been decorated for the coronation procession. Chauffeur William Webb was apprehensive as the radiator nearly boiled over, either because of the swan decoration blocking the air flow or because he had to drive slowly along the processional route. (Haverhill & District Local History Group)

Newmarket has been known as the capital of horseracing since King Charles II came to the town to enjoy racing on the heath. In the postcard picture of *c.* 1912 above the only traffic at the south end of High Street is a string of horses. At left an employee of Newmarket Urban District Council stands by his handcart. In the picture below of the High Street by the White Hart one gets a hint of the traffic problems that were to come with the advent of the motor-car; the main road from Norwich to London ran through the town.

The Rowley Mile racecourse on Newmarket Heath, *c.* 1912. (John Wilton)

The clock tower at the north end of Newmarket High Street was erected to commemorate Queen Victoria's golden jubilee in 1887. When this photograph was taken, before the outbreak of the First World War, the clock tower seemed to fit into the scene, but today it has, as Norman Scarfe puts it, 'merely been turned into a traffic roundabout'.

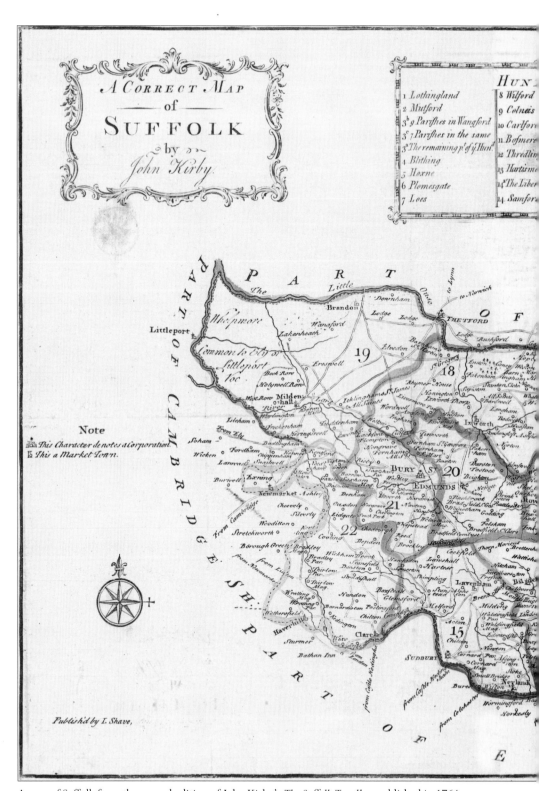

A map of Suffolk from the second edition of John Kirby's *The Suffolk Traveller*, published in 1764.

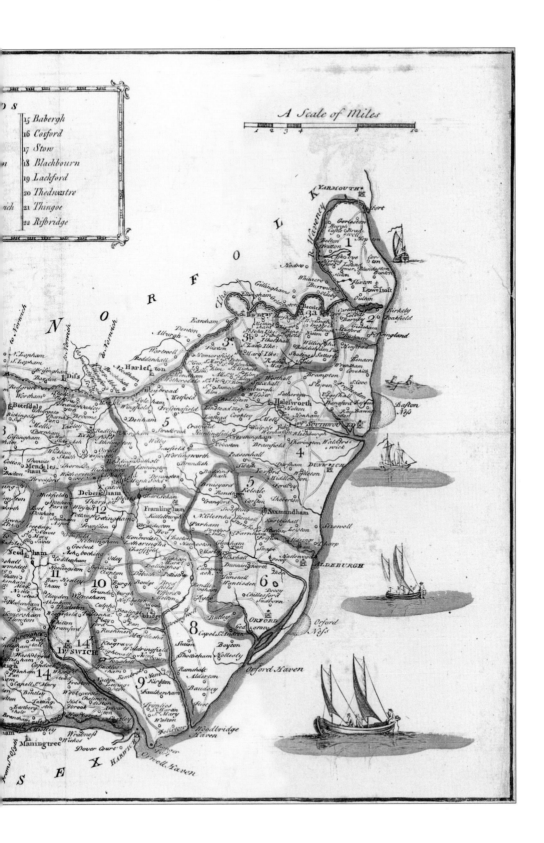

A Scale of Miles

INDEX

BRITAIN IN OLD PHOTOGRAPHS

To order any of these titles please telephone our distributor, Littlehampton Book Services on 01903 721596
For a catalogue of these and our other titles please ring Regina Schinner on 01453 731114